Big
Science Ideas

What is a Carnivore?

Bobbie Kalman

🌱 **Crabtree Publishing Company**

www.crabtreebooks.com

Big
Science Ideas

Created by Bobbie Kalman

Author and Editor-in-Chief
Bobbie Kalman

Editors
Reagan Miller
Robin Johnson

Photo research
Crystal Sikkens

Design
Bobbie Kalman
Katherine Berti
Samantha Crabtree (cover)

Production coordinator
Katherine Berti

Illustrations
Barbara Bedell: page 17
Katherine Berti: pages 23, 26 (tree)
Bonna Rouse: pages 4, 20, 21
Margaret Amy Salter: page 26 (sunlight and underground)

Photographs
© BigStockPhoto.com: pages 8 (top), 11 (bottom), 19 (top), 20, 24 (top left), 27 (bottom)
© Dreamstime.com: page 27 (middle)
© iStockphoto.com: pages 6-7, 14 (top), 15 (top), 23, 30, 31 (top)
© 2008 Jupiterimages Corporation: page 13 (top), 15 (bottom)
© ShutterStock.com: front cover, back cover, pages 3, 4, 5, 8 (bottom), 9, 10 (bottom), 11 (top), 12, 13 (bottom), 14 (bottom), 16, 17, 18, 19 (bottom), 21, 22, 24 (top right), 25, 27 (top and background), 28, 29, 31 (bottom)
Other images by Corel, Creatas, Digital Stock, and Photodisc

Library and Archives Canada Cataloguing in Publication

Kalman, Bobbie, 1947-
    What is a carnivore? / Bobbie Kalman.

(Big science ideas)
Includes index.
ISBN 978-0-7787-3274-7 (bound)
ISBN 978-0-7787-3294-5 (pbk.)

    1. Carnivora--Juvenile literature. I. Title. II. Series.

QL737.C2K34 2007   j599.7   C2007-904233-3

Library of Congress Cataloging-in-Publication Data

Kalman, Bobbie.
    What is a carnivore? / Bobbie Kalman.
        p. cm. -- (Big science ideas)
    Includes index.
    ISBN-13: 978-0-7787-3274-7 (rlb)
    ISBN-10: 0-7787-3274-6 (rlb)
    ISBN-13: 978-0-7787-3294-5 (pb)
    ISBN-10: 0-7787-3294-0 (pb)
    1. Carnivora--Juvenile literature. I. Title. II. Series.

QL737.C2K25 2007
591.5'3--dc22
                                    2007026956

Crabtree Publishing Company

www.crabtreebooks.com   1-800-387-7650

Printed in the U.S.A./03013/SN20130122

Published in Canada
Crabtree Publishing
616 Welland Ave.
St. Catharines, Ontario
L2M 5V6

Published in the United States
Crabtree Publishing
PMB 59051
350 Fifth Ave., 59th Floor
New York, NY 10118

Published in the United Kingdom
Crabtree Publishing
Maritime House
Basin Road North, Hove
BN41 1WR

Published in Australia
Crabtree Publishing
3 Charles Street
Coburg North
VIC, 3058

Contents

Living things

Animals are living things.

All living things need food.

Food gives living things **energy**.

Animals need energy to grow.

They need energy to move.

They need energy to stay alive!

Animals need energy to fly, swim, run, and jump. They get energy from food.

Kinds of food

Animals eat different kinds of foods. Some animals eat mainly plants. Some animals eat mainly other animals. Animals that eat other animals are called **carnivores**. Many kinds of animals are carnivores. This owl is a carnivore.

All cats are carnivores. This leopard is eating a rabbit.

Predators and prey

Many carnivores are **predators**. Predators hunt and eat other animals. The animals that predators hunt are called **prey**. This antelope is a lion's prey. The lion is its predator. The lion is hunting the antelope. The antelope does not want to be the lion's dinner. It is running for its life!

Small carnivores

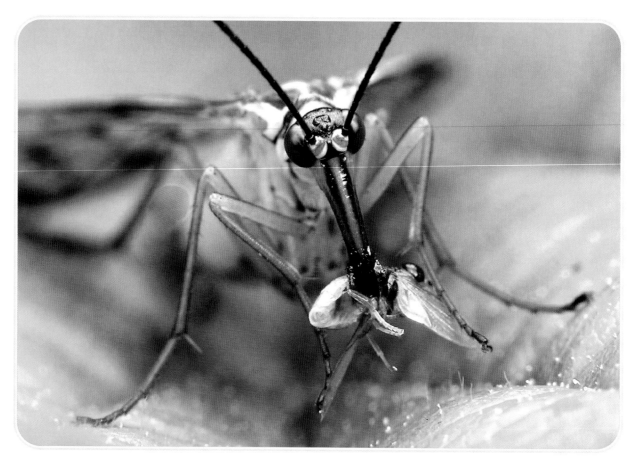

Some carnivores are big animals. Lions and tigers are big carnivores. Other carnivores are small animals. **Insects** are small animals. Some insects eat other small animals. The fly above is eating a smaller fly.

Dragonfly carnivores

Dragonflies eat flies, butterflies, and bees. This dragonfly is eating another dragonfly. Dragonflies lay their eggs in or near water. They often rest on flowers, looking for insects that feed on **nectar**. Nectar is a sweet liquid found in flowers.

Spider predators

All spiders are carnivores. Some spiders eat insects and smaller spiders. Some big spiders eat lizards or mice. This black jumping spider has caught a cricket.

Spider webs

Many spiders spin webs. Their prey get caught in the webs. The spiders wrap their prey in silk. They then bite the prey and pump a liquid into their bodies. The liquid turns their prey also into liquid. The spiders then drink the liquid.

Fishy carnivores

Not all fish are carnivores, but many are. Piranhas are small fish with razor-sharp teeth and strong jaws. They eat other fish, insects, worms, and frogs. Piranhas can clean the **flesh**, or meat, off their prey in just a few minutes.

Big sharks, big teeth

There are small sharks and big sharks. The shark below is a small shark called a leopard shark. Sharks eat many kinds of fish. Big sharks also eat dolphins, sea turtles, and seals. Big sharks are the **top predators** of oceans because no other animals hunt them.

Predator frogs

Frogs eat mainly insects. Frogs have long, sticky tongues. When a frog sees an insect, it rolls out its tongue. The insect sticks to it. The frog then pulls the insect into its mouth.

14

Frogs wait until their prey is close.
They then catch the prey quickly.
This green tree frog sees an insect
nearby. It will catch the insect
before the prey can get away.

15

Snakes and lizards

Snakes and lizards belong to a group of animals called **reptiles**. Most reptiles are predators. Snakes are predators. Some snakes kill their prey with **venom**, or poison. Some swallow their prey live. Other snakes choke their prey. They then swallow the prey whole.

This brown snake is swallowing a big rat.

This snake is a green mamba. It is one of the most poisonous snakes in the world. The green mamba lives in Africa.

Lizards are reptiles, too. Some lizards are small, and others are huge. Most lizards are carnivores. Komodo dragons are the biggest lizards in the world. Some are longer than most cars!

Tegus are lizards that eat mice, rabbits, and other small animals.

'Gators and crocs

alligator

Alligators and crocodiles are huge reptiles. These predators can eat very big prey. They can hunt and eat animals as large as deer or zebras! The alligator below is hiding in a **swamp**. It waits for prey to come into the water.

Under water

Alligators and crocodiles wait under water for a long time, until their prey comes close. They then grab the prey with their sharp, pointed teeth. They do not chew the prey. They rip chunks from it and swallow the pieces. The crocodile above has caught a big fish for lunch.

crocodile

19

Birds that hunt

Many birds hunt other animals. Birds eat insects, worms, and fish. Some birds eat frogs, mice, and rats. Most birds that are carnivores, such as these birds, catch prey with their beaks.

This bird has caught a baby mouse for its dinner. It holds the mouse in its beak.

Raptor claws

Birds that catch prey with their feet are called **raptors**. Owls, eagles, and hawks are raptors. The feet of raptors have sharp claws called **talons**. Raptors see well and hear well, too. They can spot a fish or a mouse from high in the sky.

This hawk is holding a rat in its talons.

Cats are carnivores

There are many kinds of cats. Cats that are not pet cats live in the **wild**, or in nature. Tigers, lions, leopards, cheetahs, and cougars are wild cats. All cats are carnivores. This leopard has hunted an antelope and dragged it up the tree. The leopard will have enough food to eat for a week.

Big teeth

Cats have sharp teeth called **canines**. They grab their prey and bite them with these teeth. The ridges on the roof of a cat's mouth help hold prey inside the mouth. The tongues of cats have ridges, too. The ridges help tear meat apart.

canines   ridges

This lion has killed an antelope with its sharp canines.

Wild dogs

Wolves, coyotes, jackals, dingoes, and foxes belong to the dog family. All these wild dogs are carnivores. The animal eating a mouse is a red fox. The white dog is a dingo.

*Wolves live and hunt in groups called **packs**.*

Coyotes and jackals

Coyotes, such as the one shown above, live in North America. Jackals, shown right, live in Africa, Asia, and Europe. Both coyotes and jackals hunt birds and small reptiles and mammals. These wild dogs also eat animals that other carnivores have hunted.

Energy from the sun

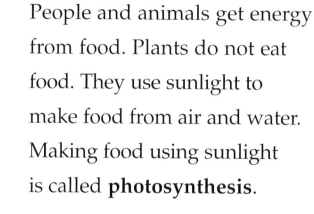

sunlight

air

water

People and animals get energy from food. Plants do not eat food. They use sunlight to make food from air and water. Making food using sunlight is called **photosynthesis**.

This acacia tree has made food from sunlight, air, and water.

Sun to plant

Plant to herbivore

Herbivore to carnivore

Plant energy

The energy of the sun is in this acacia thorn tree. When a giraffe eats the leaves of the tree, the sun's energy is in the giraffe's body, too.

Passing energy

Animals that eat plants are called **herbivores**. Giraffes are herbivores. Carnivores eat herbivores. When a lion eats a giraffe, it gets the energy of the sun and of the acacia tree. It also gets the giraffe's energy.

Food chains

Energy passing from one living thing to another is called a **food chain**.

27

Cleaning up

Food contains **nutrients**. Nutrients are parts of food that keep our bodies alive. When living things die, some nutrients are left in their bodies. **Scavengers** get nutrients from dead animals. They also help clean the Earth. Without scavengers, dead things would pile up. Vultures, gulls, and hyenas are scavengers.

This gull is eating a dead fish.

This wildebeest was killed by lions. The lions ate much of the animal and left the rest behind. Hyenas and vultures are eating the leftovers.

The last bits

When scavengers feed on dead things, they leave behind parts of animals, such as bones. **Decomposers** break down these leftover parts. As decomposers feed on dead animals, they also leave behind nutrients. These nutrients become part of the soil or water. Dung beetles, earthworms, and some ants are decomposers.

Dung beetles clean up animal waste. This beetle is rolling waste into a ball. It will eat some of it and take the rest back to its home.

This ant is eating parts of a dead beetle.

Did you know?

This Venus flytrap has trapped a fly.

Many animals are carnivores, but did you know that there are plant carnivores, too? Carnivorous plants cannot get enough nutrients from the food they make, so they eat insects, spiders, frogs, and even mice. Venus flytraps, pitcher plants, and sundews are all carnivores.

This bee has become pitcher plant prey.

Prey stick to the sticky hairs of the sundew plant.

Very important

Do you know why carnivores are important? Without carnivores, there would be too many herbivores. Herbivores might eat all the plants in an area, and then there would not be enough food for other animals to eat.

Too many deer!

In some places, there are too many deer. Wolves eat deer, but there are not many wolves left. Deer get into people's gardens and eat their flowers, fruit, and vegetables. They also eat the bark off young trees. Trees soon die without their bark.

Glossary

Note: Some boldfaced words are defined where they appear in the book

carnivorous Feeding on animals

decomposer A living thing that breaks down dead plants or animals

energy The strength to use one's body; the power needed to move and grow

food chain A pattern of eating and being eaten

herbivore An animal that feeds on plants

nectar A sweet liquid inside flowers that insects eat and bees use for making honey

nutrient Food that is needed for growth

photosynthesis The use of sunlight by plants to make food from air and water

reptile An animal with a backbone, cold blood, and scaly skin; alligators, crocodiles, lizards, snakes, and turtles are reptiles

scavenger An animal that collects anything that can be eaten; scavengers eat dead plants and animals

swamp An area of land covered by water

top predator A big predator that is not hunted by most other animals

venom A poison found in the bodies of some snakes

Index